SUNBURNED
PIGS AND OTHER TRIVIA

12-22-18

It has been my honor to know you! I look forward to our talking.

Advice: Step out of comfort zone; take control of your life - Keep humility & add being you - regardless of others' opinions!

Peace & do good for personkind,

Love,

Be true to self

SUNBURNED PIGS AND OTHER TRIVIA

Leadership and Sundry Thoughts

Dr. Maria M. Shelton

iUniverse

SUNBURNED PIGS AND OTHER TRIVIA
LEADERSHIP AND SUNDRY THOUGHTS

iUniverse books may be ordered through booksellers or by contacting:

iUniverse
1663 Liberty Drive
Bloomington, IN 47403
www.iuniverse.com
1-800-Authors (1-800-288-4677)

Because of the dynamic nature of the Internet, any web addresses or links contained in this book may have changed since publication and may no longer be valid. The views expressed in this work are solely those of the author and do not necessarily reflect the views of the publisher, and the publisher hereby disclaims any responsibility for them.

Any people depicted in stock imagery provided by Getty Images are models, and such images are being used for illustrative purposes only.
Certain stock imagery © Getty Images.

ISBN: 978-1-5320-5943-8 (sc)
ISBN: 978-1-5320-5942-1 (e)

Library of Congress Control Number: 2018912028

Print information available on the last page.

iUniverse rev. date: 10/15/2018

PREFACE

This book begins with funny title, but encompasses poignant life experiences from birth to present. Everything from children, alcoholism, family, wolves, politics, chickens, bulimia, misogyny, PTSD, pigs, harassment, bond, divorce, heartbreak, marathons, doctorate, death, dismissal, depression, Glock 19, leadership, and sexual assault, in no particular order. From personal life, book shifts to 30+ leadership lessons, learned the hard way and in some cases, not learned and finally, wraps up with "Thanks for Stopping By." Oops, I failed to mention abundant humor abounds throughout book or at least, I think it is abundant! Enjoy!

Dedication to Janie Cadena, my oldest and best friend!

ABOUT THE AUTHOR

Janie Cadena writes....

What can I say about Maria? We have been friends since we were teens. There was gap of years as we went in different directions with our lives. She went on to earn her doctorate and become very successful in education field, which is no surprise to anyone who has known her. She is a fireball who doesn't allow anyone or anything to get in the way of her goals, as evidenced by her success.

Maria is a great friend as long as one can appreciate her forthrightness! I laugh to myself as I write this because that is one things I enjoy. It also goes right along with her wicked sense of humor. You can't be her friend if you are a namby-pamby, she wouldn't allow that. She wants people to have an opinion or policy and that makes her a great leader. What a great role model she makes!!!

Courtney Criswell writes....

My aunt Maria is one of the most influential people in my life. Her love for humanity and education never cease to amaze me. Her passion for promoting equality and diversity were established within my own values at a very young age. Maria has spent most of her life educating young people on the importance of leadership. She once told me, "If you do not stand for something, you will fall for anything." Maria brings out the best in people who have the drive and initiative to succeed. Her motivational efforts to see people prosper have no boundaries. She inspired me to attend college and because of her continued support, I am currently pursuing my dream in becoming a health care provider.

It is my absolute pleasure to preface this book and I hope the people who read her story become encouraged by her inspirational views on life.

Kyla Williamson....

My aunt Maria has served many roles in my life, but I find her most notable roles as being my mentor, my friend, and my biggest fan. I'm forever grateful for diverse opportunities she has exposed me to and for her commitment to making education a large part of my life. Maria loves openly and accepts all types of people wholeheartedly (with the exception of Trump and UT fans) and she has never known a stranger. Maria has dedicated her life to leadership, education, Texas A&M University, and helping others. It is my honor to preface this book in my aunt Maria's name. May all those who read it understand her commitment and dedication

Matt, Kayla, Maria, Courtney. Texas A&M Legacy Foundation Luncheon

CONTENTS

INTRODUCTION

Should pigs wear sunburn protection? Should pigs wear hats? Should pigs wear sunglasses? Should we do more for pigs, besides eat them? Read book to learn reason for title: <u>Sunburned Pigs.</u> Smile!

The first part of book details my different life, important leadership trivia and closing thoughts. Leadership points aren't trivia, but I liked the way it sounded with <u>Sunburned Pigs!</u> Book is candid, honest and insightful. Humor, a leadership must, is generously included.

CHAPTER ONE

Bumpy Beginning

I, Maria, (pronounced Mariah) was born in San Antonio, on October 7, 1947. Upon leaving hospital, it was pouring rain, so my Dad (Webb) went to get car, but instead of picking us up he went to beer joint. Three hours later he returned drunk and drove us home. Mom and I were rain soaked, though I don't remember details. My early life was bumpy, but extended family facilitated smooth sailing.

Maria on barrel horse

My early life was enhanced by grandmothers, great grandmother, great grandfather, and great aunt; I stayed with them while Mom was working, as a nurse, six days a week. Let me explain what I gained from them, besides love. They all were major "encouragers," while life at home was very difficult. Mom did her best, but it was a tough existence.

Maria backyard

From Granny, my Dad's Mom, I learned to love reading. Every day she would lay down to read and I did too. I vividly remember going to the book mobile because Somerset had no library. Even though Granny was very bright, she had little formal education, but I could open a dictionary and call word, after word, to her almost indefinitely; her vocabulary was unbelievable. Another love I garnered from her, was a tremendous respect for the earth; her yard looked like it was landscaped by Master Gardner; indeed, it was, Granny. Finally sense of humor distinguished her from most others; she absolutely saw humor often and everywhere. No one or subject was immune. And humor is probably the primary gift I have, even though some might disagree. I even make myself laugh!

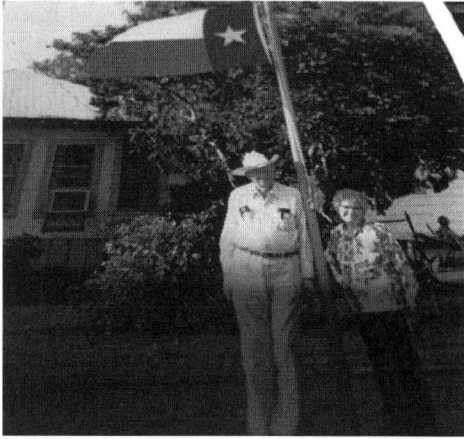

Nano & Dado, grandparents

My maternal grandmother, Nano, was quite different from Granny, but she instilled, in me, the "drive" to excel. She worked at San Antonio's Kelly Air Force Base; there, she had "top clearance" for government affairs. All I know was she worked with computers, in the 50s, when mainframe occupied an entire large room. Other than that I have no idea what she did. She too, was very bright, and expected the same from her eldest granddaughter. She either loved or disliked you; there was no gray area. For example, when Shelton (ex-husband) and I married, she went up to his parents and said, "For the life of me, I don't see what Maria sees in Jim." She never met them before; thankfully, his folks were classy enough to ignore comment. What a great segue way to marriage.

At Kelly Air Force Base, Nano made good money therefore, we shopped in San Antonio. There, she bought clothes from the Vogue and Frost, both high end department stores. I don't know of anyone else, besides Nellie, who shopped at those stores. Nano favored smart, classy suits; the same thing I wore in my career, though shorts and t-shirts are the preferred look today.

My great grandmother, Grandma, was a kind, loving woman. Besides her demeanor, she cooked amazing food and like Granny, loved plants.

3

I remember the back porch had shelf after shelf, of ivy and other greenery, all of which grew abundantly because of her love. In fact, when someone married, they borrowed her plants for the church. As was typical of the 50s, she always wore a dress, gloves and hat, when she went out. Her uplifting words and spirit permeated her home. My sophomore year, I got home and called out to her, but there was no response. I found her in bed, comatose; she apparently suffered a stroke. I called ambulance, my aunt and rest of family. For being a high school sophomore, this was a tough time. She died two days later. At the funeral, the priest compared her to Somerset's four giant oak trees: sturdy, straight, steadfast and strong, a wonderful metaphor.

Moving on in terms of family, I want to tell about my great grandfather, Granddaddy, the best male I ever knew! He truly was a Renaissance man: strong, integral, honest and intelligent. He always took the high road; for example, when the Somerset Catholic Church was built, Mexicans were relegated to the back rows, but he took a stand and sat with them. Furthermore, he indicated he would continue to do so until they were allowed to sit anyplace they wanted. It only took a couple of weeks before they were welcome in the entire church. In retaliation, the KKK burned a cross on his front yard, for supporting Mexicans.

Grandma & Granddaddy, great grandparents

Plus it was Granddaddy who got me interested in politics; I remember our watching the 1952 Republican National Convention, where Eisenhower was selected as presidential candidate. Granddaddy carefully explained current events; plus we read newspaper together with his elaborating on the in's and out's. As a result, I earned both a bachelor's and masters in political science. Plus if I had to do it again, I would go to law school rather than pursue a doctorate. Too late now.

Another significant person was Nellie, great aunt, who remained single her entire life. She was one of the first to graduate from Our Lady of the Lake University; ironically decades later I served as provost there.

Aunt Nellie

Teaching elementary school was her life's career, which left for absolutely spoiling me. She, like her parents, was abreast of current events and politics. She taught me reading, numbers and colors, providing a giant head start for kindergarten and subsequently first grade. Like her parents, Grandma and Granddaddy, Nellie was a wonderful, loving person and probably too kind for her own good. I deeply regret the numerous times I took advantage of Nellie's goodness and generosity; there was literally nothing she wouldn't do for me. For example, Nellie bought me a brand new Pontiac, Le Mans, the coolest car at the time. Several years later, she got me a new Pontiac GTO, with racing stripes. She was comfortable financially, but certainly not up to purchasing two expensive, new cars. Again, I shall always be sorry for taking advantage and being disrespectful to her. She clearly deserved better.

At the time of Nellie's death, I lived in Michigan, and remember being called that she had passed away. I flew home and handled funeral arrangements. I did all the things I thought she would want, but when it was over, I opened her purse and found detailed notes and very little, of what I had done was what she wanted. I remember breaking down, upon finding the notes. It was the last thing I did for her and failed. But I know she would say, "That's ok, Darling, you did your best! Her tombstone reads "She loved others."

CHAPTER TWO

Lord Be with Her, if She is Stupid

I must relate my first day at St. Mary's Catholic School, as Mom loves to tell the story. Parents were standing outside crying, leaving their babies for kindergarten, the old "empty nest syndrome." Anyway, when I looked up and saw Mom crying, I asked her to leave because she was embarrassing me. That story of independence pretty well summarizes my life: smile.

St. Mary's Catholic School took me when I was five years old, but moved me into first grade quickly thereafter. There were probably two reasons I was moved into first grade: 1) I knew the kindergarten curriculum because Nellie taught me; 2) I was a little demon. Let me explain; I loved to cruise around the classroom and visit with everyone, but the nun told me to sit down, which I failed to do. She put me in my chair, untied bow on my dress and tied me to chair; it was hell pulling chair around.

Here is another antidote on St. Mary's Catholic School. The nuns lived in a convent next to school, so we climbed up the wooden fence to check their clothes line. You might ask why we went up the fence to check clothes line; it was to see if any undies were hanging on the line. In other words, we wondered if nuns wore panties under their habits. Keep in mind, nuns' hands, feet and face were all that were visible; otherwise they were totally covered, by habit. Today, I can't remember if undies were there or not. Rats!

After finishing Catholic second grade, I wanted to attend public school, but there was a problem. Mrs. Koch, third grade teacher, was known for disliking Catholics so Mom went and visited with her to determine if she would treat me fairly. When asked, Koch responded, "If Maria is smart, it will be fine, but Lord forbid if she is slow." So it was a 50-50 chance. Mom gambled and I became Koch's "pet." I even got invited to her house and brought along a friend. My charisma, charm and humility paid off. Ha.

A couple of other things I remember: Gary, my cousin, lived next door and we got into lots of trouble together. Once we were playing with matches and burned wooden fence down. Another time, we climbed under Daddy's model A and filled every hole with dirt. Surprisingly we weren't killed; we got into massive trouble other times, but with these two events nothing happened. Another thing that comes to mind is once we were playing Cowboys and Indians; Gary hid in a tree and captured me; he said to throw my pistol up. Well, I tossed the play gun up, but he missed and it hit my head; I bled like a stuck pig. Finally we often played with table knives and I got stabbed in the hand and still have a scar from that incident. In summary, I grew up tough, a great lesson for life! P.S. I had a doll, but never played with it. To my way of thinking, today's kids are shielded too much; life is a constant struggle, so why sugar coat it? Why give everyone an award when life only rewards winners? Shouldn't children learn competition is necessary to survive?

CHAPTER THREE
Pretty Full of Myself

Jumping ahead to 7th grade; I was elected class president and gave everyone jobs: straightening books, cleaning up, etc., But in so doing, I learned a vital thing about leadership; treat others with respect. I was pretty full of myself; however, in 8th grade, I failed to be elected class officer, a real disappointment. So I spent year showing others respect and was elected class treasurer all through high school. Sidebar: Later in varied leadership roles, I failed to remember the lesson and relearned the hard way.

Because Somerset was a small South Texas town, we had a tiny school district, meaning there were lots of "big fish in a little pond." I got in band in 6th grade because the high school band needed people and I continued through high school. My junior year, I tried out for drum major, beating out two girls who were thought to be favorites. Here, I learned something else; people get angry when they think they deserve something and you get it instead. Both of them and several of their friends dropped out of band. Plus, they and their families spread horrible gossip like, my parents paid off the superintendent so I could be drum major; little did they know my parents had no money. Another bitter reminder occurred when I went to Sandra's house, one of my good friends. Bernice, grandmother to one of losers, lived next door, and every time I went, she hollered out "Frankenstein," despite my looking nothing like him. Smile.

Something else I realized, only Whites were in high school band. Hispanic girls participated in pep squad. It never dawned on me blatant discrimination was the reason for non-participation. Plus the two races never dated; it was against the social more of Somerset. Not only was prejudice prevalent in music and dating, but no Hispanic was ever elected class officer or any club leadership role. Additionally Latina females never played sports.

My senior year was largely a waste of time; there were no advanced placement classes; in fact, there was only one elective: Homemaking. Only boys took FFA, so we were stuck in Homemaking, which speaks to expectations for females. We only had one high school English teacher, the superintendent's wife and she seldom showed up for class. When she did, she put on makeup. Obviously she got by with it because her husband was "boss." In four years, I never saw her stand and teach; she simply had us complete workbooks and as a consequence my writing skills were nill. In fact, it was in doctoral work where I actually learned to prepare an outline, write and review. Pretty sad. Needless to say, I struggled in freshman English and got two D's, but was tickled to pass.

At this juncture, I must relate a Homemaking story. The teacher told Janice, friend, and I to stay after school and knead bread. We had no clue what that meant and when dough rose we used spatulas to beat it down. Well the beatings lasted over an hour and bread kept coming back; we tired of activity and went home. Needless to say, teacher looked at dough the next day and asked what happened to it; we told her we couldn't keep dough from rising. Can you believe we didn't make a high grade for after school work?

Also during my senior year, the band director quit or was fired; who knows? Anyway, rather than hire a substitute, the superintendent told me to take over all k-12th music and band classes; remember, I was drum major. So for six weeks, I attended none of my classes and directed k-12 music/band classes instead. Needless to say, the superintendent informed my teachers that I was to make straight A's, while I was out. At the time, I never questioned the decision; can you imagine that happening today? No way! P.S. I don't remember any trouble carrying out the job.

Further, my favorite high school course was government, taught by the high school principal. I fell in love with subject, ultimately majoring in politics, for both Bachelor's and Master's. If I had to do it again, I would go to law school in lieu of earning a doctorate, but it's a tad late now. Sidebar: The principal took me to Texas A&I College, to pursue scholarship and we met with the dean. I had no idea what a dean did, but I remember walking into his office and stuck out my hand to shake hands. When he stood up, he had no hand. What do you shake, in that circumstance? Ha.

Changing subject now, something memorable happened my senior year. I met a young man on a blind date and remember thinking, "I hope no one sees me with this guy" because he was thin and pale. Plus, no one introduced him and I was too embarrassed to ask his name; our friends said something about Shelton so I thought it was his last name. Three weeks after we had been dating, he asked why I called him by his surname. I told him I thought it was his first name and he said his first name was Jim. Well in that period of time the name stuck. Not only did I call him Shelton, but my entire family did, as well. In spite of our breaking up off and on for four years, we married for 22 years. More on topic later.

CHAPTER FOUR
A Troubled Man

At this point, I want to talk about my father; a World War II Marine whose military job was establishing communication on the Japanese Islands prior to Marines landing. In four years, he experienced lots of action. On one island, he and his best friend were in a foxhole; unfortunately his friend was hit in head. When Daddy removed his buddy's helmet, it was filled with brain remains. I simply cannot imagine Daddy's fear, angst and anger.

Daddy

Another horrible thing happened when Daddy contacted malaria and nearly died. He remained in hospital a full year; when my grandparents were initially notified, there seemed to be little hope of his leaving hospital. So for a whole year they thought he had died. Because letters were heavily didacted, it was impossible to learn much of what was happening. Keep in mind there were no cell phones and emails, at that time.

Also, remember, the war fear permeated the United States, eventually resulting in Asian Americans being imprisoned in camps. Their homes and resources were taken, leaving them with nothing. German Americans weren't locked up because they looked like "Americans." Crystal City, Texas had a Japanese internment center, if you ever get close, about 100 miles from San Antonio.

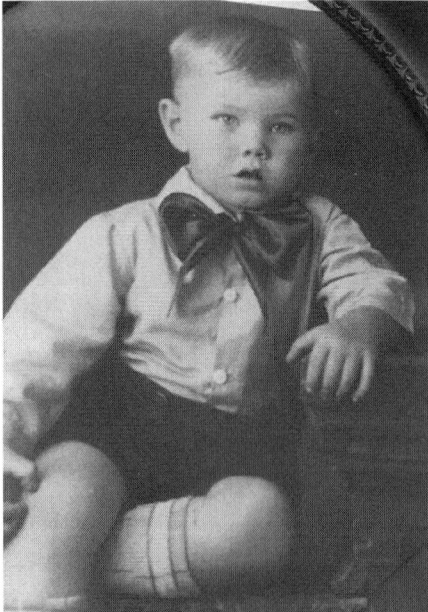

Daddy, baby picture

Sadly, post-traumatic stress syndrome was unknown, at this juncture in history. Clearly Daddy received no emotional help and as a result, became an alcoholic upon his arrival home. When he was drunk, he was violent. Much of my childhood was affected by his disease, especially around Thanksgiving and Christmas holidays. One Christmas I remember his being drunk, grabbing a shotgun and saying he was going to kill a guy; my uncles literally tied him to the bed, where he passed out. Other times I recall his coming home drunk, no money and clothes torn off, from beer joint fights.

Another negative about my Dad was running around on Mom; in fact, the night I married, Mom was looking for him so he could walk me in to begin wedding. She finally found him outside with her best friend, Gloria. They were both drinking; I didn't know about this incident until a few years ago, when Mom told me. Sidebar: After my folks divorced, Daddy and Gloria married.

Another time I remember Mom finding a pack of cigarette matches, from a sleazy South San Antonio motel. When she found the matches, she said "Let's drive over there." When we got to the motel, Daddy was walking into a room, at which point, we drove away. He never knew we saw him. I was in fifth grade, at that time.

I, also, recall getting home after school and finding a hole in the kitchen wall; when I asked what happened Mom said Daddy got mad, pulled pistol, bullet discharged and struck wall. The hole was repaired, with a band aid; too bad our lives couldn't be fixed that easily.

As is typical with abusive situations, everyone "walks around on eggshells" to avoid setting off the alcohol. Daddy would get upset for no reason and yell and scream; I hated being around him because the norm was screaming and hollering. His negativity was especially bad on my Mom; nothing she did was ever good enough. One time she changed ceiling light bulb, dropped cover and split her head wide open. Daddy came in and rather than helping, demeaned her for being so stupid. I honestly don't know how she did all she did: worked six days a week, washed, ironed, cleaned, cooked and nurtured me.

On the positive side, Daddy could build and do almost anything. People loved being around him, because of humor. When he laughed, his entire body shook. At his funeral, the priest talked at length about how much he loved being around him because of humor. Isn't it a shame he never received the help he needed to live a rewarding life?

Sidebar: Besides abusiveness and alcoholism, my Dad raised and fought roosters. Not only was this illegal, but the people who fought roosters weren't the crème of the crop. Incidentally Ray Price and George Jones, country singers, often attended. The way cockfighting worked was in a small pit arena, gaffs (small knives) were tied onto roosters' legs, until one rooster prevailed. I lived in mortal fear the Texas Rangers would raid the place and throw Mom and Dad in jail. The local sheriff and constables were paid off to "look the other way" but there was no paying off the Texas Rangers. Luckily they never got caught rooster fighting, even though they were raided once. Someone drove up and hollered the "Rangers are coming;" everyone took off running with chickens in hand. Anyway, the Church of Christ preacher, who preached on Sunday mornings and fought chickens in the afternoons took off running, falling and breaking his extra thick glasses. Well he made it to his car, pulled out a fishing rod and ran over to a pond, hoping to convince the Rangers he was fishing. The funny thing was there was no water, so he was casting onto dry ground. When the Rangers arrived, they asked him what he was doing; he replied, "fishing." Smile! The chicken escaped when Driskoll went down.

To add some more information on cockfighting, handlers trained chickens by running them back and forth over a carpet, dropping them so they would fly better and feeding them very expensive food. Roosters were bred for their bloodline just like horses; expensive roosters might run as much as a thousand or so dollars and this was forty years ago. I didn't recognize until much later rooster fighting was cruelty at its best, but I didn't know what I didn't know.

CHAPTER FIVE

Your Mom Blows You Away

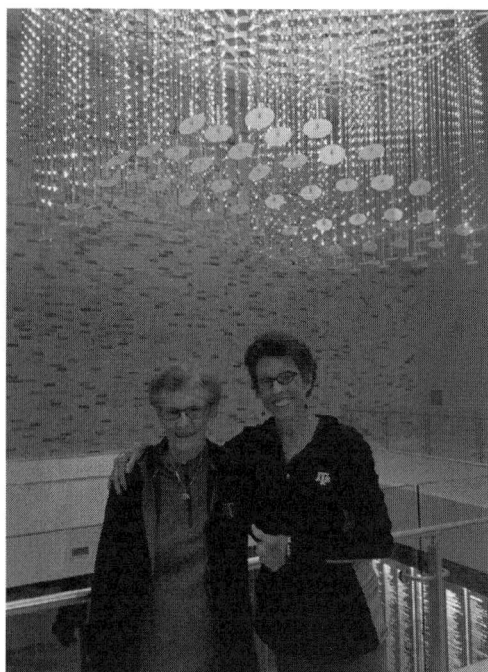

Mom & Maria at the A & M Memorial Student Center

What about Mom? I mentioned earlier she worked, as a nurse, six days a week washed and ironed clothes, cooked meals, cleaned house and fed over 20 wolf hounds, a day. The clothes washer was in backyard, so we washed dirty clothes outside and hung them on clothes line, to dry. We ironed everything: sheets, handkerchiefs, pillow cases and clothes. In fact, Nano, my grandmother, even ironed her bras, good thing they weren't mine, as they would catch on fire, with so much foam rubber. In terms of cooking, everything was from scratch: no cake mixes, no microwaved dishes and no store bought bread. If people came in house, without wiping their feet off, they were dead meat, so to speak. I mentioned 20 wolf hounds; Daddy hunted wolves; yes, there were wolves back then. A typical wolf hunt took all night, so Mom and I slept, in the back of the truck, while Daddy was hunting. I honestly don't know why wolf hunting was popular; what can you do with a dead wolf?

I said earlier that Mom and Daddy divorced after I got married. She later married Elvin, as mean a man as I ever knew. His saving grace was a little money; at any rate, he was physically and verbally abusive to Mom. Lord only knows what he did and said that I know nothing about. Shelton and I literally snuck her out of their home and she came to live with us, even then, he stalked her. I remember getting home one night and Shelton and Mom were having wine so I asked what they were celebrating. They found Elvin's obituary in paper. So I had wine too; there is no doubt, he would have killed all of us, had he not died.

Not only was Elvin abusive and mean, but he was a royal bigot. For example, Earl Campbell played football for University of Texas, one of the first African Americans to play sports at a non- traditional Black university. Anyway, we were at their house watching Texas game and Elvin went off on Campbell, calling him a baboon, ape and other derogatory names. I simply couldn't stand his racism so I confronted him; anyway we had a huge fight and Shelton and I left. I had a severe panic attack, on the way home. I don't recall ever speaking to Elvin, after that incident.

After Shelton and I divorced, Mom often went with me on business trips: Alaska, California, Florida, England, and Sweden. Yes, she paid her own expenses. She hung out with my friends, while I worked, after which they invariably said, "Shelton, you are neat, but your Mom blows you away."

Mom & Maria University of Texas game

An especially funny thing happened when we flew back from Sweden. I was on aisle and Mom was by window. A very obese man came down aisle, with huge piece of luggage and when he lifted suitcase, to put it in overhead bin, his pants hit the floor. He had no idea pants fell down, but all of us saw it and fought back laughing. Well, his "package" was right at my face level, even more reason to fall apart. What could I say? Finally someone said, "Sir, your pants fell down;" he quickly pulled them up and took his seat. He never moved until we landed in New York.

Fast forward, up until two years ago, Mom went with me to Aggie football games, where she proudly stood with 12th Man. For those unfamiliar with Texas A&M University traditions, the (12th Man) fans stand entire game, in case team needs help. And believe me, the team needed 12th Man pretty often. Note: Mom never attended A&M, but is as loyal as any Aggie!

Mom & Maria Aggie at Rose Bowl game

This is all not to say, things are perfect between us; we have ups and downs, especially the last two years. With her deafness, blindness and cardiac issues, it's been much more difficult. During same time, I suffered major health issues, largely stemming from my balance proprisception, where brain fails to communicate with joints. In other words, my body lacks awareness of where it is "in space." It is tough putting shoes on when you don't know where feet are. Ha.

Mom, Janie and Stella Marie endowed scholarship

In five years, I had three broken wrists, three broken pelvises, as well as shattered hip. Wrist, hip, foot, hand, knee and stint surgeries were required. Then a year ago I fell, shattering my mouth on concrete.

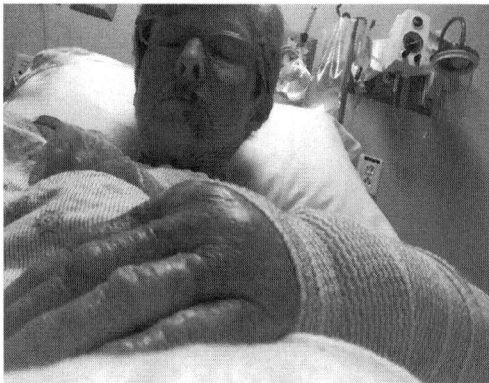

Maria after fall on cement

Here, I crushed bone holding top teeth in place; the dentist I went to should have referred me to surgeon, but instead he tried countless bone grafts and implants. After a year, I realized he had screwed up my mouth, so I went to surgeon. It was 12 months before I could eat solid food. I told Kyla and Courtney, my cousin's kids, to take me to junk yard when I died because I had so much valuable metal. Oops, I failed to mention rather than taking dentist to court, I called and told him I wanted my money back and plus, he would pay for any problems thereafter. He agreed and sent me check for $12,000.

CHAPTER SIX

Sixties and Seventies

Let me take a minute and provide a glimpse of Somerset life in the 60s. There were no computers, video games, cable news, colored televisions or cell phones; Girls wore dresses to school, even though we all wanted to wear jeans. There was no central heating or cooling; fans were our only "coolers. Moutons, faux fur, jackets were THE item to be hip. Penny loafers were favored shoes. There were no dances because Baptists outnumbered other religions and condemned such sinful behavior. However, Baptist parents had no problem with their kids going to drive in's, where "making out" was the norm. Homes weren't locked because there was no theft or burglaries and neighbors helped neighbors. Everybody knew everyone's business or at least, the gossip surrounding them. If a girl became pregnant, she left town, seldom to be seen again, while the guilty male was unpunished. Most girls graduated high school and married local boys. Few students attended college. In fact, my class of 41 students only had one female go to college: me.

After high school, I went to Texas A&I College, a small regional school in South Texas. The only reason I chose A&I was it traditionally had good football, a solid reason for choosing a college. I struggled academically because I had no background, especially in English. Remember, I mentioned having the same high school

English teacher all four years. I made two D's in college English and was never so happy for D's. Honestly I didn't learn to write until doctoral work; it could be argued I still haven't mastered writing. Smile. I also learned essays were my preferred testing mode, rather than multiple guess. So remaining years I selected professors who only gave essay exams. I made Dean's List thereafter. I failed to get smarter, but I simply figured out how to work the system.

Following two years of college, I married Jim Shelton, the "blind date" from high school. I might add I paid for engagement and wedding ring because he had no money, so rather than borrow money, I used my meager savings. He finished college and began teaching. I quit college and applied for an elementary teaching position in Edgewood ISD, the nation's poorest school district: with no degree, interview or application, I was hired over the telephone. Unbelievable!

During the 70s, Texas had no limit on the number of times a child could be retained. And as a result, the least number of retentions my second graders had was two years. I had 13 year old males, who shaved. Remember, this was second grade. Needless to say, most kids dropped out prior to graduation. And it certainly didn't help that I had no clue what I was doing. After this horrible year, I completed my degree and made $3,000 a year teaching government and economics.

As far as politics, Viet Nam War was going on and proved to be a terrific topic for government class, especially considering my kids were seniors and would be drafted after graduation, not to mention, my husband getting draft notices. We both felt strongly the War was wrong and had no intention of supporting it. Over 55,000 Americans died; thousands maimed. Sadly, the War took on racial tones when predominately minority males were drafted; Caucasians chiefly evaded the draft by employing exemptions: marriage, children, college, disabilities, etc., There were massive anti-War demonstrations and protests across the country. In fact, some Kent State students were killed during a protest. Clearly it was a divisive time, but not as bad as today. A large number of us considered the War illegal because Congress never approved it; President Lyndon Johnson simply enacted executive orders. Further, my ex was draft age and used every exemption possible, but finally, was ordered to report for a physical. We were prepared to go to Canada, to avoid the draft, but Shelton mentioned to the doctor his soft spot (head) never closed up entirely. Well, this blew the doctor away, so he had to research the issue. Thankfully, a lottery was established, during this time, with the lower numbers called first and highest numbers avoided draft. Shelton got 362, meaning it was highly unlikely he would be drafted. Incidentally medical report returned and indicated he would have to wear helmet 24-7 because if the soft spot got hit, death ensued. The War finally came to a close, with no winner being declared. I might add when Shelton got out of line, I simply thumped the soft spot. Smile.

CHAPTER SEVEN
Failure to Bond

We were married six years and had no luck getting pregnant, so we completed paperwork to adopt. One month, from the day we applied, the adoption agency called and said we could pick up our 5 month old daughter the next day. My husband and I knew nothing about a baby, but thankfully, one of our friends took us to pick up "baby stuff." The following day we drove downtown San Antonio childless and left with an infant, scared out of our minds.

Plus the adoption agency required me to quit my job so I could be a fulltime mother, talk sexism. But again, we didn't know what we didn't know. I only lasted a month; I couldn't stand being at home fulltime, so I talked the agency into my going back to work. But the school district had given my job to someone else, so I ended up teaching pregnant girls, in a stand-alone building. I learned about babies, from them.

Ok, back to being a mother, by the time we arrived home, Susie had pooped her diaper. Now remember diapers were safety pinned on, no Velcro. Well we tried to change her diaper, but by the time we finished, the diaper went under her arms. I told Shelton, the only way the diaper was going to stay up was to buy suspenders. Smile. About that time, our next door neighbor came over and offered help; she was awesome. She even showed us the "in's and out's" of diapering. On related note, Susie had dysentery one time and the only thing I could get her to eat was plums; after several days, I called doctor and was told plums contributed to problem.

On a related note, Susie was ¼ Hispanic; our families were quite opposed to our adopting a "mixed" race kid. It was over three weeks before any family members came to see her. Prejudice was alive and well and still is today, oftentimes in the name of religion. More about my thoughts on that later.

During the 70s, adoptive parents learned nothing about child: family, siblings, illnesses, etc., so we started with a blank slate. But as time went on, it became evident something was amiss with Susie; she wasn't close to anyone, including us. Now, the tragedy is labeled "failure to bond," but we didn't know and would have adopted anyway. The problem increased as she aged; I remember going to her kindergarten teacher and Susie was seated away from everyone else. When I asked why she was separated, the teacher said that was her choice. Even outside, Susie would sit by herself and fail to engage with classmates. We even had her repeat kindergarten thinking maturity might help, but nothing worked. For years, we did individual, as well as group counseling, but things worsened.

Ultimately Susie dropped out of high school and refused to work or to do anything worthwhile. I couldn't trust her and upon returning one Sunday, from teaching an out of town graduate class, the house looked like a bomb had detonated. To this day, I have no idea what happened, but decided it was her or me and I chose me. I kicked her out and changed locks; she prostituted both ways and finally her dad moved her to San Antonio. There she completed GED and went in Army, only to wash out. She wouldn't follow their commands either. She still resides in San Antonio and goes from one part-time job to another. Her Dad gives her money but, I cut that spigot off a long time ago and we aren't in contact. It is sad, but true, shit happens.

CHAPTER EIGHT

Teaching, Counseling and Leading

I moved from teaching to counseling to leading, beginning as interim vice principal, establishing an alternative K-12, serving as district summer school principal and moving into a principalship. However, I wanted to earn a doctorate, so I applied at Baylor University. But my GRE math scores were low, with high verbal skills. Baylor rejected me and when I appealed, the dean told me I was not smart enough to successfully complete a doctorate. I was devastated and spun into massive depression. I had a high undergrad and graduate GPA and was a successful principal, but she refused to budge on admittance.

About six months later, my superintendent asked me what I wanted to do when I "grew up;" I told him about my Baylor experience and he suggested I apply at A&M, a Texas flagship university. I shared the Baylor experience and told him there was no way A&M would take me. But he was an Aggie and believed in me, so I applied. Fortunately, the University looked at the entire student and body of work, not just GRE score. After three interviews, I was accepted unconditionally.

I transferred 24 hours into a 72 hour program because I already had principalship and superintendency coursework. Hoping to work smart, I immediately decided on my dissertation topic, "faculty meetings," so, thereafter, every course paper centered on that topic. I literally worked as hard as I could, taking maximum hours each semester. I always questioned my ability, but had complete faith in my chairman, Dr. Harold Hawkins. I submitted a draft and he provided feedback the next day; I then made corrections and returned the document, so he worked as hard as I did. Anyway, I finished my doctorate in two years, which may be the fastest doctorate ever earned at Texas A&M University. My friends took much longer, 4-5 years, but they didn't decide on dissertation topic and waited until course work was complete to settle on a topic. Moral to story: work smart.

Getting Johnny Manziel's autograph

Further, Dr. Hawkins mentored and coached me along the way and after I "walked," I moved into higher education. Hawkins helped me decide where to apply: Temple, Central Michigan, George Washington and Central Arkansas and was offered interviews at each university. It was the perfect time to apply because A&M's Leadership program had just been named the top American program. Plus, women were desperately needed in higher education leadership programs because few females held leadership experience. Truly, it was an "old white guys" culture where women were largely excluded, except for female elementary principals. In fact, I once applied for a high school principalship and was told I was best candidate, but wasn't big enough to paddle high school males. Again, sexism and I didn't know it. Anyway, I interviewed and felt comfortable at Central Michigan and said "yes."

Regarding comfortable, I liked the "old white guys" at CMU and it was a great fit. Here's something I learned, I loved collegiate sports, especially football and easily carried on football conversations with colleagues. Truly, interpersonal skills play a huge factor in securing and keeping job. You never know what grasps someone's attention: hobbies, travel, sports, books or whatever. For example, when I interviewed for management with AT&T, I hit it off with interviewer when we talked about marathoning; he wanted to run race and I told him how to prepare. I marathoned 15 years, with 3 hours and 45 minutes being my best time. I didn't know squat about telephones, installation and repair, but I stood out because of marathoning. Running taught me independence, toughness and discipline. Sidebar: My interpersonal skills helped me many times, but also failed me, others.

Maria at A&M, old Kyle Field

An interesting event happened the first time I attended a Central Michigan University-K12 meeting. A superintendent asked me if I were the new secretary at CMU. I told him I was the new leadership faculty member; he about fainted. They only had White guys up to my going there. Sexism often occurred, with both males and females, but it was never discussed.

Upon our moving to Mount Pleasant, Michigan, it took my ex six months to secure job because unions got insiders promoted, making it very difficult for outsiders. At any rate, he finally secured a counseling position, not a positive thing for a numbers person. By this time, he was depressed and drinking. Internal bickering became the norm for our family. In one incident, he and Susie got into it and he said, "I should leave; she replied, "Yes, you should." So he packed up and left. The following Monday he called and wanted to come back and I said no. I knew it was over. We divorced six months later. Telling him "no" was heartbreaking, but all other options had been tried; there was no feasible alternative. I knew it was just a period of time when the same or similar incident occurred again.

CHAPTER NINE
Heartbreak in T'Town

After several years, I gave up on Michigan winters and started looking for another faculty position. I applied at several institutions and received offer from University of Alabama. Even though I was hired as faculty my department chair asked me to assume program director position, as well as teach. I told him I was the rookie and position needed to go to veteran faculty member, but he said no, so I accepted job. I knew going in as rookie and instantaneously taking leadership responsibilities, would be problematic. But, once a risk taker, always a risk taker.

It was during this time, I met Ken on a blind date and fell madly in love with him. We set the wedding date, but two weeks before the event, he dumped me. If that wasn't bad enough, we went back together three more times. During one of those times, he had a Dallas trip planned and when I asked him where he was staying, I realized it was with a woman. I got so angry, I pulled him up from the recliner and literally threw him to the floor and when he got up, I put him down again. I seriously considered getting pistol and killing both of us; thankfully I didn't.

Deep depression set in; I had physically and emotionally built my life around Ken and all of a sudden, my dream was over. During this time, I had to attend a New Orleans Conference and it was there suicide nearly became reality. I remember lying in bed figuring how many pills it would take to kill me. About the time I figured out how many pills were required, I heard a knock on my door; it happened to be Jo Ann, my doctoral student wanting to go to dinner. I told her I didn't want to eat. She demanded I open the door or she would get security to take it down. I knew she would contact security, knowing how depressed I was. Thank goodness she was persistent because I wouldn't be here without her.

It's important to understand doctoral students and committee chairs are about the same age, with similar life experiences. Strong relationships sometimes form and this was the case with Jo Ann. She also had a teenager and was divorced. We had a strong bond fortified by the fact that only about 1-2% of Americans hold a doctorate and to earn the terminal degree student and chair must work closely together. Truly, she had a "fire in the belly" for success.

Adding to the depression was also the fact that invitations, wedding date, church, ring, flowers and dress were all set. In fact, my University friends held a luncheon, honoring Ken and me. My family had booked hotel and flights, but alas I announced wedding was off. Coupled with these horrific experiences, Tuscaloosa was a relatively small town where it was common to "run into people." Friends often reported where they had seen Ken which caused me to spiral even more. Eventually, my psychologist told me to tell friends not to report anymore "sightings."

Sidebar: I have dumped and been dumped and let me guarantee the latter is far worse; self-esteem and self- confidence are basically destroyed. "What could I have done differently" plays over and over. Sleeping and eating become almost impossible. Getting out of bed was so difficult because there is no reason to get up. Crying became the new norm. I made it through those six months, but it was awful.

Finally, to provide a flavor of Alabama culture, at University of Alabama, doctoral chairs "hood" their students at graduation. For commencement, I traditionally wore a suit, with regalia on top. Anyway, I had to stop for gas and when I went in store, the clerk, who saw me all the time, said, "Golly, you are all dressed up." I responded I had to hood six people, to which he replied, "Shit, I didn't know you were in the Ku Klux Klan." I told him he obviously didn't know me very well because I would never belong to a White Supremacist Group. Again, we see the ugly head of racism and bigotry.

CHAPTER TEN
Fun and Sun and More

Affected by personal and university experiences, I decided to leave Alabama and take job at Miami's Barry University. Change of scenery helped tremendously except Barry proved to be horrible place. I was quickly promoted to associate dean, but the female dean made life a living misery. She never trusted anyone, especially me; she went through my desk over weekends. When I suspected what she was doing, I purposely set desk contents in special way and if items were moved, I knew she had been in my desk.

Besides distrust, Sister Evelyn treated people terribly. For example, we attended a campus meeting together and she demeaned and yelled at me, in front of other administrators. I didn't say anything at the time, but as soon as we were outside I told her to fire me or write me up, but never, ever treat me like that again.

One other time, a faculty member, a nun, confided in me about her depression and wish to kill herself. I told Sister Evelyn so we could get the nun therapy, but instead Evelyn said "Shit, if she kills herself, we will have to do another faculty search." I was absolutely blown away with her lack of caring and concern.

Fortunately, Ft. Lauderdale's, Nova Southeastern University, called me to interview for dean of educational leadership. Even though I had only been at Barry six months, I went for it and was offered the job. There, the situation was totally different: great provost, administrators, faculty and students. Plus I was first female to hold the position, a trend that happened over and over. Nova proved to be the best and most exciting time in my life. We simply rocked.

Nova had an excellent reputation, but doctoral program lagged behind in technology, staff development, student mentoring and coursework. The "good old boys" started the program 20 years earlier, but little changed. For example, there were no female or minority faculty; none of the courses were updated; there was no technology and female students suffered sexual harassment at the hands of the "old white guys." The females were told, if they didn't have sex, then they would never graduate. Unfortunately, sexual assault exists in terminal degree programs because one professor can, indeed, prevent dissertation from being approved and student graduating. Students never complained because no one believed them; sounds like today: Weinstein, Cosby, Trump, Dr. Ford, etc.

Upon learning about sexual harassment, I cleaned house. Men, who did this were fired, but they created quite a bit of trouble, as they bombarded president about being with program and suddenly being dismissed by first female dean. When, my boss, and I met with University Vice President, female, I might add, she suggested we compromise. Well, my boss and I hit the ceiling; how is compromise considered when such egregious behavior happens? But, my boss and I prevailed and the "creeps" were gone. The changes cost me some political capitol, but it was the right thing to do.

Also, we opened job searches, especially hoping for excellent females and minorities, such that would mirror student population. Because I had been president of two national professional associations, I had excellent network and we brought in some dynamite folks. Students were so pleased knowing some "wrongs" were being corrected.

In terms of course updates, I met with senior lecturers and asked what updates they were planning; the ones who didn't see need for change, were gone and replaced with contemporary professionals. The law course was 20 years old and never revised. Can you imagine? I hasten to mention some senior lecturers stayed and made great changes and helped us recreate culture. They also counterbalanced the dismissed guys and provided continuity.

As far as technology, I brought in folks who knew what we needed and they provided subsequent training to students, faculty, administrators and lecturers. The folks in the trenches, made super suggestions; they knew where the weaknesses were. Anyway, technology kicked off in D.C., at our summer conference. It was so exciting; we had set up hundreds of computers, in the hotel and conducted training there. P.S. I participated in each session, as it was vital to show I was "walking the talk."

Sidebar: Two really funny things happened at the conference. One, when I completed the keynote speech and started down the dais stairs, my heel got hung in the cuff of my pants and off I went. I heard a collective audience gasp, but got up and said, "I was checking to see if you were paying attention." The audience fell apart and I was teased about the fall for years. The other experience also involved me. I took stairs to avoid waiting for elevator, but when I tried to open the door, it was locked. I screamed and banged on door forever and finally realized I had to pull fire alarm to get door open. As I emerged from stairs, I heard firetruck sirens and found fire fighters evacuating the entire hotel. I never told anyone I caused the alarm to go off. Sometimes you just have to do what you have to do. Ha

At the end of the first year, significant advances were in action, but lots still needing doing. The former dean established a connection with Swedish university administration, though nothing was done. I saw a possible way to take our program international and provide our provincial doctoral students with a look into the future: best practices of major universities. Initially, we met with Swedish administrators in New York City and brainstormed possibilities. They were very open and supportive; I knew we would learn much from them and vice versa.

In addition, the Berlin Wall came down in 90s, but professors, from former communist countries, had little exposure to the states. Plus, they had no money to attend conferences; we set up 10 scholarships and those scholars conducted sessions and participated in ours. I truly wanted us to hear their experiences, providing an unbelievable opportunity for us and them. They chaired sessions and we gained so much from these amazing scholars.

At this point, I emphasize culture changes didn't happen because of me. Charlie, my assistant dean, had no problem telling me when I was heading into a rabbit hole. I didn't always like what he said, but I always listened and reconsidered. Plus our staff was stellar, especially Johnnie and Sheila, who had been with the program, since its conception. They truly loved program and wanted only the best for it. We formally recognized them at the University of Uppsulla, where summer conference was held. The two women received a standing ovation and deserved so much more. Their trophies had their names, with tenure dates, as well as thanks for job well done. There wasn't a dry eye, in the auditorium. Sidebar: policy and courses are important, but without people, there is no heart and soul! Always remember: people first.

Besides Charlie and staff, our office manager, Moisette, was brighter than all of us put together. Like Charlie, Moisette left no doubt where she stood. She had been at Nova about four years, as a clerk. After I had been at NSU a few months, I saw tremendous potential and promoted her to higher position. At that time, she only held a high school education, from Montreal, Canada. I encouraged her to begin Bachelor's degree at NSU; she was hesitant and apprehensive she couldn't handle the academics, but graduated, with Honor's. She soon finished her Master's and began doctoral work. She notified me a couple of months ago she is now Dr. Moisette; I am so proud; sometimes it just takes someone to believe. Sidebar: Believe and encourage others; it is the most important legacy. There are lots of rough diamonds out there.

Dick, my boss resigned after I had been at NSU four years. I literally would have walked on fire for him. He epitomized leadership: people oriented, high expectations, entrepreneurial, supportive, positive, creative, and risk open. There was no pretense about him; he knew who he was. Unfortunately, he and the Vice President clashed; yes, the one who wanted to compromise about sexual harassment. She wanted him to become a traditional, bricks and mortar provost and this wasn't his style. When I received the call he stepped down, I cried and I cry very little.

A new provost was hired, Miles, and we hit it off at first. In fact, he created a new position for me, assistant provost. Things went well for a few months, but then crashed. Miles' wife, Martha, also worked in the College; in fact, she ran the show; he only had the title. She and I got crossways spelling the end of my time with NSU. He called me in on a Monday and said he was eliminating my position and I was history. Thankfully, Dick had extended my contract six months before he left so my salary and benefits continued during that time. Also I hired an attorney known for taking care of dismissed Nova employees; he got me another year of salary and benefits from the

University. I must say it was very traumatic being terminated, my first such experience. All of a sudden, I lost University friends because they were afraid the same thing would happen to them. It is telling, the staff were the ones to set up a dinner to honor me; no faculty or administrators showed. Fear truly prevails.

CHAPTER ELEVEN
Licking My Wounds

When position is eliminated, self-doubt and fear take over. Not only was my leadership position gone, but most of my friends were too. Plus, my status was gone; I finally kicked myself in the butt and established a leadership consulting firm: coaching teachers who couldn't teach and leaders who couldn't lead. Luckily, my network paid off, as many Florida administrators were former students and they knew I had lots to offer. I contacted every superintendent and principal I knew and told them what I was doing. My schedule filled up and I worked each day. I thoroughly enjoyed this time because coaching folks and making a difference felt great.

I might add working by myself was challenging; I always interacted with people, but following elimination, I worked alone. The loneliness was depressing. Plus, many of my former NSU friends didn't want to chance their being cut, so I was "persona non grata."

Another item was difficult, cash flow. I never knew when I would get paid. At one time, Broward County Schools owed me $26,000 and I had monthly bills to pay. Anyway, I gradually adjusted to working alone and learned the import of putting money back for "rainy days."

CHAPTER TWELVE

Kyla and Courtney, My Heartbeats

After several years, I decided to move back to Somerset to be close to my cousin's kids, Kyla, third grader, and Courtney, first grader. I loved them and wanted to be part of their lives. We went all over Texas, visited both California and Florida, picked out books, bought computer and followed school events. I wanted them to love learning, respect diversity and recognize a cosmopolitan world, outside of Texas. In all honesty, I also brainwashed them on being Texas Aggies.

Maria & Courtney posing

During the time, I was back in Somerset, I served on a school facilities committee. At the time, an elementary school was partially complete, but languished from board and administrative logjam. Indeed, the school was two years behind schedule. Also at the time, the board fired superintendent, leaving position open. The board president and I developed a positive relationship and he wanted me to take superintendent's job. He had a terrible reputation in Somerset: crooked, mean spirited, and evil, but I thought I could work with him. Boy, was I wrong. In actuality, he ran school district, hence reason for leaders being fired.

The board was split: five with president and two opposed. Needless to say every vote was 5-2. There was no concern about kids, even though sides argued they were looking out for students. Two board members lacked high school educations and neither kept their own electricity turned on because they didn't pay their bills. And there I was with leadership doctorate and they were telling me how to manage 500 employees and $35,000,000 budget. I received board members' emergency calls about cheerleader uniforms and basketball socks. Gradually the president infringed upon my responsibilities; some days I received 15 calls telling me to do something. He, also, expected to have immediate entry into my office, regardless of whom I was seeing.

No doubt board president had emotional issues, in fact, he probably was bipolar. There were days when he burst into my office hysterically crying. Then other days, he demonstrated bizarre, inappropriate behavior. For example, when a board member's father passed away, he clapped, danced and cheered, at the funeral. Everyone turned around to see what he was doing. Plus board president was hitting on the assistant superintendent calling her with obscene, suggestive messages; unfortunately, she refused to report it and there was nothing I could do. When we went out of town, she and I would trade hotel rooms, in fear of his coming into her room. In reflecting, she may have been going along with the affair and stabbing me in the back, all the while. Needless to say, she became superintendent, when I stepped down.

Further, I knew my days were limited so I documented everything; I believed board members received money for supporting certain building contractors. In fact, the two members who couldn't keep electricity turned on, suddenly drove very expensive trucks. And there were other strange things happening while massive building projects continued. There was lots of money being spent, a ripe recipe for embezzlement.

Finally I decided to take my 28 pages of documentation to Texas Education Agency (TEA), hoping they would investigate the board and especially the president. The board constantly usurped my superintendent domain. By state law, school boards made school policy and superintendent carried out those policies. But, Board was oblivious to the obvious demarcation. At any rate, TEA came to the next board meeting and commended Board on well they worked together. I was devastated that none of my documentation was considered. So I wrote my resignation letter and submitted it to board president. Guess what, the board vote was 5-2, so they let me out of contract. I didn't ask for any money because I wanted money going to kids, not me.

CHAPTER THIRTEEN
A Fatal Mistake

But I had a backup plan; an old friend of mine was Our Lady of the Lake (OLLU) University president and when I was going down at Somerset, I met with her, for possible job possibilities. It turned out the provost position was open and I had necessary credentials. We were both interested in making it happen, so I signed contract for interim provost job. I left Somerset on Friday and started at OLL on Monday. By the way, contract gave me more than $30,000 increase over superintendent salary. All was roses, so it seemed.

The University had serious problems: College of Education had no idea if they were in the black or red. Declining student enrollment, old coursework, staid faculty, bureaucracy and too many administrators prevailed. For example, there were four administrators over technology and no technicians. In other words, no one repaired University computers or software. But, the most urgent item was probationary status with Southern Association of Colleges and Schools (SACS). If we failed to get off probation, we would lose accreditation meaning no Pell Grants (loans), for our students. In other woods, University would close.

I met separately with key faculty, administrators and students to gain insight; I asked lots of questions and said very little. Rather than detail everything that happened, I want to speak to the biggest leadership mistake I ever made. Of all the problems, none was worse than School of Education, where dean was very weak and there was no definitive budget numbers. I ultimately dismissed dean and opened search for position. There was an insider, who had been dean, at one time, I found her very capable, but caustic, negative and critical and on the other hand, I knew she would fix key issues in the College. I ultimately hired her as dean, but her negatives quickly arose.

The Education dean treated her peers and me negatively. She was constantly criticizing; in fact one day she came into my office and handed me a list of 20 items she felt I had messed up. Never, in my life, had I had employee do such a thing. After I read list, I moved her out of dean's job, but I made two fatal mistakes: 1) University president was out of town and I failed to keep her abreast of problem/dismissal, a huge no-no in leadership; 2) I didn't issue any announcement to faculty, staff and students, so fired dean shaped discussion in her favor, another huge mistake. Anyway, her supporters went crazy with criticism and faculty was threatening a vote of "no confidence" in me. Such a vote had no binding power; it was simply a political ploy to make me look inept. By this time, our president returned and I told her I wanted to step down as provost and move to faculty position. I panicked; I couldn't sleep or eat. But the president said I let her down; she wasn't alerted/consulted and I had "duped" her. Plus if she couldn't trust me, she didn't want me on faculty. So I was quickly out of a job. I wrote a letter of resignation and submitted my keys. Her refusal to move me to faculty caught me totally off guard. I was a full professor, top of the heap, but it made no difference. And here, I made another error; I didn't send out an announcement to staff, faculty and students, so she shaped public opinion. People were shocked; a provost never stepped down and I had. It made me look bad. I will always feel badly about how I handled dean personnel issue, but quitting, without fighting, I regret. I always told students to fight adversity, but I stepped down out of fear of rejection. Plus I overlooked what I always told students; keep boss informed on major issues/problems.

In spite of totally mishandling a key personnel issue, we accomplished a good bit: gained full Southern Association of Universities accreditation, for five years. The entire staff worked so hard to make it happen. In addition, we totally reorganized technology department and budget; a number of administrators were released and replaced with technicians to keep computers going. Plus, we instituted across the board technology training for staff, faculty and students. We developed a process for simple repair/update of all software and hardware. We signed an agreement with major tech company to develop software for students needing additional assistance. Plus we painted dorms, replaced old mattresses and redid murals, something that had not been done in 20 years. I hosted dinner for entire faculty and staff, at my home, a real morale booster. I might add one female custodian, who regularly cleaned my office, was so excited her group was invited; I made a point of fixing her plate and waiting on her. Unfortunately, she unexpectedly passed away three weeks later, but I was so happy she received respect she deserved. Plus we recognized others for outstanding service, something that never occurred.

CHAPTER FOURTEEN
Two Reasons for Living

To reinforce the import of education, I drew up a new will, stating Ky and Court would receive 25% with bachelor's, 50% with Master's and 100% with doctorate.

Courtney, Kyla & Maria

I didn't want their getting money, without working for it; plus I wanted them to earn at least one degree. Strategy worked; Ky acquired bachelor's and Master's and Court finished bachelor's and began physician assistant graduate program this week. Needless to say, I am very proud of these young women and only hope they spend their lives helping, learning, being inclusive and enjoying a great big world.

Kyla at wedding shower

Kyla before her wedding

As I stated earlier, I didn't do a good job of "mothering" Susie; career was clearly my priority and we often relocated for job promotions. The more mobile we were, the more difficult it was for Susie to adjust. I hate being this honest, but it is true. Recognizing the hard fact is probably why I took such an active role with Ky and Court. Of course, I played an ancillary role with these kids, but still take credit for pushing education and their standing up for themselves. I, also, know there were times I embarrassed them when taking a stand, but life is hard and I wanted them ready for adulthood. Sidebar: The Four Agreements is still my favorite book; check it out; it made a difference in my life.

Further, the high point in our relationship was June, 2013, when I took them to Europe for Ky's bachelors and Court's high school degree. I figured this would be the only time we could make it happen, given their work, school and my health. They picked where they wanted to go: Ireland and England and I surprised them with a Chunnel trip to France. Knowing we would self-destruct given too much time together, I got two hotel rooms. I told them up front they were adults and trusted them to behave accordingly. Sidebar: They made me proud, just like The Self-Fulfilling Prophecy: people act according to the faith shown them.

Maria giving Kyla her Aggie ring

Two especially funny things happened on our trip. Ky and Court had a spat so Ky decided to take a nap. Court cruised over to my room, but when she left their room, she turned the maid sign around to request cleaning. So the maids went right in, with Ky in bed and not much on. Needless to say, Ky was pissed. The other thing was when I told them I wanted to spend the day alone taking pictures and reading. They both voiced concern about my being ok and finding the hotel. I assured them I was fine, as long as I had American Express card. I had had three knee surgeries, two major within 4 month period. Both knees were wrapped and I was gimpy, but managed to have great day. I never told the kids I had trouble finding the hotel; they still don't know. But with credit card, I knew I could always get cab. Smile.

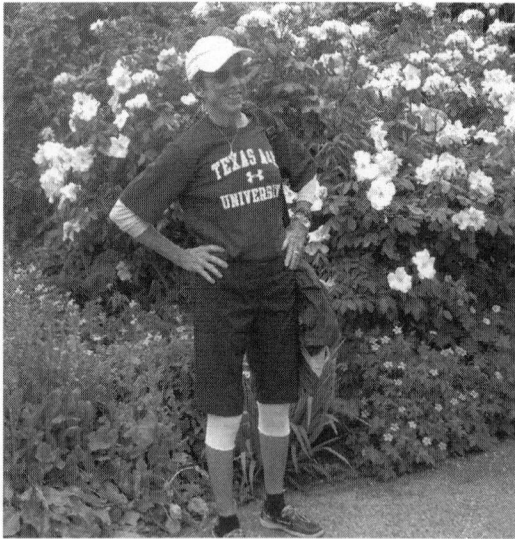

Maria, gimpy in London

The Europe trip was something we will always cherish; the kids were on the cusp of their lives and I wanted them to experience the world outside Texas, to respect diversity and to be inclusive. In my opinion, the greatest education is travel; no class provides the transformative equivalent. Nothing replaced the look in their eyes when they first used subway. Nothing replaced the look in Court's eyes when she recognized drinking age was 18 and she could, indeed, get wine. Nothing equaled the look in Ky's eyes, when we literally pushed her into crowded subway. She insisted some guy grabbed her rear end; I would love to have someone grab mine. Smile. I am so thankful we had this special time together!

Kyla and Courtney, sleepy in London

Kyla, Maria & Courtney, Tower of London

CHAPTER FIFTEEN
Petey, my Soulmate

More recently, I moved back to Austin, for the third time, but this time, I took up rowing, kayaking and making amazing friends, who shared those passions. One such special person was Pete (Petey) who at the time was married, but whose wife died shortly thereafter, from cancer. She only lasted one month, after diagnosis. Petey and I were great friends and even greater, after his wife passed; up to that time, it was strictly friendship, but morphed into love. The first time I stayed over, Pete went to linen closet to get towels and when he opened the cabinet, there was Judy in an urn. I about fainted and he had no idea she was there. He yelled at son for not taking her to San Antonio. My knees just about buckled; what can be said? We were together about six months, but he wouldn't take the next step for fear of what his son and daughter-in-law would think. They thought I was after Pete, for his money, little did they know, I had more. Smile! I grew tired of status quo and moved back to West Coast Florida, after which, Petey and I again grew close.

Bradenton, Florida proved to be a disappointment; it was sub-tropical with extreme heat and cold. Plus, my health was terrible; in one year, I was told I had cancer, as well as had three knee surgeries, two major. Plus, it was like going to Padre Island, Gulf of Mexico. It clearly wasn't anything close to Ft. Lauderdale, a true tropical paradise, with warm winters and pleasant summers. Additionally, it was politically conservative, totally unlike Ft. Lauderdale. Finally I failed to make significant friends; it was a pretty lonely time. So, I decided to buy a small home in College Station, Texas to be there during football season. I planned on keeping West Coast condo, but liked College Station, so I sold Florida property. A year later I bought a large, new home in Aggieland. I have now been here five years, but am considering moving back to East Coast Florida; I truly miss ocean, tropics and "blue" area.

Relating back to Petey, our relationship centered on love, common interests, landscaping and politics. When I got call from one of our mutual friends, I immediately feared something was drastically wrong; Somers simply said, "Pete died." Petey and I talked constantly about moving in together, but we waited too long. So now at night, I tell him how much I miss and love him and Winston, his English Spaniel. There is a huge void in my life without Petey; he was truly my soulmate. Moral to story, don't procrastinate when relationship is positive; we never know what tomorrow may bring. In our last conversation, Petey said "Maria, you know I love you," to which I replied, "I love you too."

Maria & Petey

Not only did I lose Petey, but his son gave Winston dog, to a virtual stranger; I told his son my Cavalier and Winston played together and I would love to take him. I was even more heart broken after losing Petey; Winston lost his Dad, home and went to someone who virtually didn't know him. I knew Petey wanted me to have Winston, but his son was an ass.

Austin friends celebrating Pete's birthday. Maria far right

Let's move now to the present situation; I think about moving to East Coast Florida for several reasons. One, College Station is a tough place to live because it is comprised of mostly married, conservative couples. Two, there are no bodies of water except for several lakes, filled with speed boats and drunken individuals, neither of whom do I choose to be around. Remember, I kayak and motorboats "wake me". Finally, since Trump became president, the Christian red necks emerged in full strength; there is little room for liberal, inclusive discussion. I simply cannot see how educated, successful friends condone Trump's sexism, misogyny, homophobia, and zenophobia, but they do. And what's worse, they sit in church every Sunday, never questioning their elitist biases. I don't recall Jesus condemning people's gender identification, sexual orientation, social economic status, age, religion or race. Truly, the worst atrocities occur in the name of religion; for example, Crusades, wars, degradation of women, disabled, and minorities etc., Finally, no fair and loving God allows horrific events like hurricanes, earthquakes, starvation, disease, suffering, fires and war where millions and millions of innocent people succumb.

On a more positive note, I advocate for Sexual Assault survivors, both male and female. I took over 50 hours of class and on-the-job training to qualify and find it very rewarding; I now have purpose in my life, something I lost after kids grew up.

CHAPTER SIXTEEN
Leadership Trivia, But not Really

At this point, I move from personal and professional life, to "Leadership Trivia, those points I learned and experienced over my career.

P.S. The title, <u>Sunburned Pigs and Other Trivia</u>, derived from my tenure as superintendent. At that time, Somerset ISD was a poor district, but the school board approved extending a building roof to protect white pigs from being sunburned, a costly non-academic addition. Construction cost over $100,000 and those monies could have gone for academic improvements, but board determined white pigs were priorities. You have to love it, only in Texas.

Leadership Trivia is a series of unranked commandments I gleaned over the years or in some cases failed to learn. Nonetheless, leadership commandments aren't trivia, but I liked the way it sounded with <u>Sunburned Pigs.</u>

1. Laugh at yourself; others will certainly do so. In other words, avoid taking yourself too seriously; we are tiny dots along a long span of history. My favorite "laugh with me" story is when I fell off the dais, after delivering keynote address, to over 1,000 people. They were shocked, as well as video

person, who later told me, "You were there and then you were gone." When I got back to my feet all I could say was, "I wanted to ensure you were paying attention." Everyone laughed and I turned bright red.

2. Treat others as you want to be treated. Every leadership role I held, I made special effort to know custodial, cafeteria and maintenance people and take time to visit and to see how things were going. Those folks always had my back; they truly cared about me. No organization functions without hardworking employees, yet they seldom receive recognition, respect or appropriate salary. Therefore, treat all employees just like the president of the United States, though not the current administration.

3. Listen twice as much as speaking and avoid changing discussion to yourself, when others talk. I need to work on this every day because I prefer to talk about me. And "listen" denotes more than hearing; watch body language, which is what people actually feel.

4. Establish and maintain eye contact; failing to do so signifies lack of self-confidence. I never hired someone who avoided eye contact; I found them untrustworthy. Note: Steady eye contact is essential when confronting someone, whether it be store manager, employee or employer. Avoid the "blink."

5. Good strong shakes are a must, no "Charlie, the Tuna" shakes. Like eye contact, hand contact conveys confidence and respect. It's important to initiate handshake and control the other person from overpowering. Think of Trump, not only does he initiate, he pulls the other person into his space. I had a high school principal who grabbed hand to pull person off balance. In so doing, he established control.

6. Dress for desired position; in other words, dress so others visualize you in the sought after position. Avoid over dressing; a kindergarten teacher shouldn't wear stiletto heels. But, attire sends clear message of values and attributes.

7. Obtain needed certificates/licenses prior to open position. For example, I completed counseling certification before actual opening and then when job opened up, I applied and got job. Another example, I completed principal certification and when position arose, I was hired. Finally, I earned superintendent's certification and when superintendent was fired, I was ready. Note: Having paperwork doesn't ensure getting position, but it makes a statement.

8. When encountering an angry person, use "I" language, rather than "you" or "why."

   For instance, if confronting a teenager who skipped school, say "I am very upset you skipped school," rather than "Why did you skip school" or "You really screwed up."

   There is nothing to be gained by using "why" or "you" because the language puts other person on defense. Express feeling by beginning with "I."

9. Related to irate individual, encourage person to elaborate. For example, when parent blames teacher for child's misbehavior, encourage adult to elaborate and when she finishes talking, ask if there is something else to add. Eventually person will calm down and be open to discussion, but it might take a while. I must admit as long as I dealt with conflict, I never mastered it. I ruminated prior and post episode.

10. Something else I learned was to rehearse prior to going into conflict. Use a trusted confidante to role play and practice what will be said and what might come up. Ensure the person is trustworthy or it might blow up in your face.

11. Also regarding conflict preparation, reflect on the absolute worst thing that could happen, even though it seldom occurs. The same practice strategy is applicable when prepping for a job interview.

12. Moving into a totally different subject, meetings, I have lots to say because it was my dissertation topic. So much time is wasted; so much morale is destroyed; and so little is accomplished in common meetings. Here are some ideas to improve meeting efficacy.

    1) Determine if meeting is necessary; could email accomplish same thing?

    2) Establish purpose of meeting; what is the goal?

    3) Set questions up to accomplish the purpose. For example, how could we improve student registration? What could we personally do to enhance student experience?

    4) Solicit agenda questions from staff members, but ensure items enhance meeting purpose. If employee contributes question, then that person should introduce the item.

    Also avoid having more than 15 participants.

    6) Oops, I forgot to mention a very cogent meeting point; no one talks more than 2 minutes, including you. Place a toy train on table; ask someone to keep time and when someone exceeds two minutes, then timekeeper pushes toy train over. Oftentimes the folks, with oral diarrhea, monopolize discussion. Don't allow this to happen.

7) If any meeting participant remains silent, ask question to solicit input.

8) At top of agenda, place date, place and time; beginning and ending time. Also state meeting's purpose/goal. Avoid punishing punctual folks by waiting on latecomers. If someone consistently comes in late, then have one-on-one session. If someone is doing something else, like texting, one-on-one.

9) Summarize meeting discussion/decisions, especially review duties different folks might have, at meeting end.

10) Finally, hand out index cards and ask participants to complete: To me, this meeting was.......Meeting could have been improved by......Folks are free to sign or to not sign index cards; have a basket where cards can be placed. If a card/s cites criticism, discuss or respond at subsequent meeting.

Here is a great example of criticism yielding improvement; at one meeting, a person wrote she hated the way I played favorites with one person. When I reflected, I realized the criticism was true. There was banter between two of us, excluding others. At next meeting, I apologized and stated it wouldn't happen again. At the end of year, the person confessed she was the one who wrote criticism and really appreciated the fact I changed behavior. So the moral to story is evaluate, because ineffective meetings kill moral.

11) Depending on leadership role, sometimes speaking to media is necessary. Here are a couple of suggestions: Avoid saying "no comment." Have in mind the point/s to be made and reply to questions with those thoughts. Watch CNN or other major network and see how interviewees respond to questions; it is clear what their talking points are. Good

leaders avoid "rabbit holes" because they become "sink holes." When failing to answer or not wanting to talk, simply say the matter is being investigated and an announcement will be forthcoming. Always be courteous to media regardless of situation. If interview is prearranged, wear simple jewelry and professional attire. Close off interview with key talking points.

On a related note, provide several positive messages/ announcements each week, to make up for uncontrolled "oh, shits." Finally determine who is authorized to speak to media and who isn't.

13. Remember politics exists everywhere: family, synagogue, church, mosque, school, or government; so don't be surprised when it "raises its ugly head." Harold Lasswell (2010) defined politics as the "study of who, gets what, when and where." Resources are inherently limited, hence people battle to garner a piece. Being naïve and assuming folks are out for the common good is ludicrous. I don't care if they are spouses, friends or partners; expect deception. For example, when school board voted to spend money on a roof for pigs, it wasn't about animal welfare; rather, it was for gleaning election support, from FFA students' parents.

14. Moving on, let's speak to health. In high profile environments, there is a ton of stress, necessitating exercise, eating healthy, emoting, maintaining finances and employing spiritual practice. Being an old jock, I exercise, but with three major knee surgeries, hip replacement, three broken wrists, one foot surgery, heart stint, two breast biopsies, and two hand operations, it has been tough. Most surgeries resulted from balance proprisception, where brain fails to communicate with joints.

15. Additionally, I have depression and when I can't exercise, depression crops up. Let me say, yes, I am on anti-depression medication and when doctor suggests stopping medicine, I change doctors. Truly, there is still a stigma about mental issues, like something is wrong with person. When someone questions my depression medication, I tell them if I had strep throat, I would immediately take something and also remind them you can't talk yourself out of "feeling low." Depression is a brain imbalance and can be either hereditary or causal or both. The recent suicides of Robin Williams and Anthony Bourdain speak loudly for getting help. Finally, when appropriate, I share my struggle with others, so they seek assistance, when needed.

Next on the list is eating healthy. What we eat definitely affects our wellbeing: physically, emotionally, financially, socially, and spiritually. I became a vegetarian and avoid red meat and greasy food, mainly because a virus settled in small intestine and acts up when I eat certain things. Decide what works, in terms of diet, and do something that makes sense.

At this point, allow me to share another major health issue; I have an eating disorder, (bulimia) common for female, Type A, oldest, and only children. When leaving AT&T, I never dreamt of having difficulty getting another job, but Affirmative Action became law and minorities were sought. I hit rock bottom; in fact doctor wanted me to go in hospital, but I refused. Every day I took entire box (30) of Ex-Lax, so remainder of day was spent on toilet. Ironically, I weighed more with eating disorder (134 lbs) than ever before. Cake was my trigger; I bought, hid, and ate all of cake, when family was sleeping. Then my weight went up, which necessitated additional Ex-Lax. With much therapy, hypnosis, and medication, I gradually escaped bulimia, but recognize relapse is possible, just like with alcohol and drugs. By the way, males also experience eating disorders, but less frequently than females.

Moving on, emoting is essential in leadership; just be cautious who confidant is. Besides speaking with someone, journaling is helpful; for others, yoga, therapy or meditation prove beneficial. Truly, there are days when even your Mother doesn't love you. Smile. The higher the position, the more people criticize. It's like being in a fish bowl, without water. Just remember to keep a calm demeanor regardless of situation. As saying goes, "Don't let them see you sweat." Easier said than done, right?

Turning to finances, avoid using company/school credit card, instead use personal card and submit receipts for reimbursement. Many leaders find themselves in deep water, when using company credit card because if there is a mistake, they are blamed. Also avoid putting liquor on credit card; generally institutions won't reimburse alcohol. Finally a personal story, I was named superintendent and bought a new Lexus, my enemies claimed school district paid for it, which was a total falsehood.

Also maintaining personal finances is vital; recognize net income and keep within those perimeters. Regularly invest money and pay off credit cards. Get savings taken out of check before spending or you will probably never invest. The home mortgage should constitute no more than 30% of monthly expenses. As you probably know, trading a car when money is still owed doesn't make loan go away; old debt simply adds to new loan. Finally, avoid binge spending as it generally occurs with stress, anger or chaos.

At this point, determine what decision-making filter is employed; in other words, upon what basis, will decisions be made? For me, the bottom line was what was best for students. Remember, politics arise when resources are limited. Regardless, consistently use decision making filter that exemplifies values and beliefs.

Moving to another point, avoid "duck poop," where someone comes with problem (poops) and expects you to handle it. Rather than stepping in poop, ask individual what should be done? By refusing to step in poop, the person takes responsibility and grows as a result. Even though poop theory is somewhat funny; the reality is leaders personally enable co-dependency, when handling poop, rather than fostering leadership others' leadership.

Coinciding with "duck poop" is "open door" policy. Here, leader announces door is always open. Never, never make this a practice because it encourages co-dependency. Even though it sounds positive, it is a terrible mistake. I saw many leaders fail as a result of poop and open door policy; their time was consumed with minutia. Avoid these missteps.

As mentioned earlier, a huge part of leader's job is fostering staff growth and professional development. Training must be proactive, not "sit and get" sessions. And it is imperative leader participates so message is believed. Here's example; I received call from principal who had no rapport with staff and they were threatening walk outs, so I visited with principal and several key staff members. We determined what should be done, in terms of training. The session went great, except principal didn't attend so nothing was accomplished. Staff said "See this is typical" and reason for no team spirit. I went to principal's office, only to find her doing paperwork.

I told her I was very upset; her absence demonstrated her lack of commitment. By the way, I told her I wouldn't do anymore training.

16. We spoke about leadership and there are many such theories, mostly worthless, but here's one that works. Rensis Likert's (1976) "Linking Pin Theory" postulates effective leaders serve as "linking pins" between different organizational social groups: maintenance, custodial, secretaries, supervisors, human resources, and accounting. When a group is angry or ineffective, check and see if they are involved in communication or if they are overlooked. For example, when I was principal, the cafeteria workers were constantly complaining and non-productive; when I thought about it, they had no say or input into policies, even though policies impacted their everyday work lives. So I changed processes to ensure they were actively "linked" and their attitude and outlook turned positive. Clearly, "Linking Pin" worked in every leadership job I had; when communication broke down, a group was out of loop and I had to "link" it to other social groups.

17. Another helpful theory is Gouldner's (1957) study where people fall into one of two groups: "Locals" who largely remain where they grew up and are committed to the culture, while "Cosmopolitans" see the world as their habitat and thrive in other cultures. Most folks are Locals; far fewer are Cosmopolitan. The reason I am sharing Gouldner's work is organizations require both types of people; Locals maintain culture and traditions, while Cosmopolitans bring in new ideas derived from other cultures. Personal note: Over the years, I grow bored when I stay in one place five years or so. In fact, I am looking at moving to Florida's East Coast now. I thrive on doing and seeing different things.

18. Shifting from leadership theories, I want to emphasize import of staying away from negative people; as the old Texas saying goes, "She would be negative, even if hung with a new rope." Dark humor! I have several friends who don't see the glass as half empty; they don't even see the glass. Smile. In fact, one of them is at her best when she goes to a funeral; she repeats the lurid detail until someone changes subject. I make a point of warning new employees to avoid negative people because they suck the breath out of life by debasing staff, community, students, parents and administration. I might add working with negative people is problematic for me; I simply have no patience with them. I always feel like telling them to "suck it up and get over it."

19. Furthermore, talking about people, remember "no good deed goes unpunished." By this time, you are probably thinking I am negative, but life is tough and just because something positive occurs, expect few thanks and appreciation. In fact, when good things happen, people simply demand more.

20. On another somewhat negative note, avoid using school cell phone because everything is subject to public information request. I recognize paranoia seems rampant, but enemies will go to any lengths for revenge. I saw people followed to see if they were having illicit relationship; pictures were taken. Finally, assume everything on internet or computer is public information. For example, when I stepped down as superintendent, board had technologist check my computer hard drive to see if I had anything that could be used against me. Never put anything controversial on school computer.

21. Talking about computer, here is a very interesting story. As university provost, we had tech issues at night; sometimes entire system went down. Our technology department

checked everything, but couldn't find cause. Eventually they thought problem stemmed from library. Coincidentally, there was a librarian who kept office locked during hours, with him inside. No one remembered ever seeing him help anyone, but former administration did nothing, so he continued. Anyway, we suspected he was downloading porn, causing system to crash. So university police, technical director and myself went and knocked on his door. He didn't want to open the door, but we told him we would take down door, if he failed to unlock it. Upon checking, technology director, I and police found tons of child porn. It seems he downloaded at night and watched during the day. Needless to say I fired him and police promptly arrested him. The point is he had been at university over 20 years yet no one followed up on why he was seldom seen.

22. Moving to confidentiality, avoid sharing secrets even though it is tempting because it's fun telling others and folks love knowing it. The biggest temptation is confiding in a trusted friend; simply don't do it. As is readily apparent with Trump administration, trusted friends turned on him to protect themselves.

23. Upon assuming a new position, invariably someone asks, "Will you back me?" A friend gave me the perfect response; "I will back you unless you do something illegal, immoral or stupid." The statement clearly sets necessary boundaries as well as elicits laughter.

24. Something happened to me one time, but it is important to share. I worked with a superintendent who appeared inauspicious, but was brilliant. He supervised my internship and one day mentioned he was retiring at year's end, but to keep it confidential. At the time, my ex also worked in same

district and it was very tempting to tell him, but I didn't. Superintendent had no intention of retiring, but he knew if he heard someone say he was leaving, it was me who leaked it. He purposely set me up to see if I could be trusted. Always be on guard.

25. The same superintendent employed the "divide and conquer" strategy to keep staff from uniting against him. He pitted one person/group against others so people were afraid to cross him for fear of what he might do to them. Strategy worked, he kept his job over 15 years, a rarity in today's superintendent's world. On the national level, Trump employs same strategy; one person/group is criticized making others afraid to complain. "Divide and conquer" works, but ultimately kills staff morale, with most employees ultimately resigning or quitting. Occasionally this phenomena is called "Chaos Theory."

26. Let's turn now to documenting; make notes of anything weird or out of place. Cite date, time, place, subject/s, participants, and discussion. For example, when I went to Texas Education Agency, I had 28 pages of single spaced accounts citing board/members' infractions. I gave a copy to TEA and kept original. To my knowledge, the Agency never investigated the matter, rather they took board side and blamed me for problems, even though every superintendent for 30 years was fired by board. Odds are there couldn't be that many incompetent leaders in a row. Note: Use personal, not organization computer; store info on private thumb drive and keep it at home. Also when documenting, write immediately after event occurred. A good example was James Comey, fired FBI director, who wrote notes, following meetings with Trump. His accounts were immediately written up, adding credibility to documentation.

27. Changing subject, I want to speak to interviewing. I had disastrous interviews and I had amazing interviews. An example of the former was when I applied for public information officer; I got actual job confused and kept speaking about another position; it wasn't until after interview I realized I messed up. Needless to say, I was so embarrassed and there was nothing I could do. But the extraordinary interview was a piece of art. In planning, I asked if interview was by one person or committee and it was the latter. I learned everything I could about the organization: history, records, failures and successes. In addition, I prepped every question I could think of and thought out responses. I also practiced interviewing with a committee of friends who provided invaluable, honest feedback. I wore professional, navy blue suit, low heels, modest jewelry and makeup.

In prepping, I also planned answers to questions like: What is your greatest weakness? What would former employer say about you? What would you do on first day of work?

What is toughest personnel issue and how was it handled? What is your biggest failure?

What skeleton is in your closet? How would you learn about organizational culture? What would you do if employee came up and began criticizing organization? What is your greatest leader attribute? Give me an example of your building a team culture. Why do you want this job? Why are you leaving your current employer, after only six months? How much money do you want?

Because it was a committee interview, I considered shaking hands with just the chair or with everyone. I decided to shake hands with all members, carefully calling them by name. Hint: When I went in room, I jotted down names and seat locations so when I responded to a question, I could say Dr. Brown, I ....They never noticed I had sketched layout prior to beginning, so they thought I instantly remembered each one's name, an awesome coup.

After the interview, I again shook hands with each member and thanked them. I also wrote each one a personnel note, thanking them again.

Oops, I forgot the funniest part. I had lunch with university president and regent. Well, lunch was broiled chicken; I immediately knocked entire plate onto my lap. The only thing I could think of was humor, "I was just checking to see if you were paying attention." We all laughed and went on with lunch. I guess they figured if I could get through that debacle, I could handle anything. Thankfully, I got job.

28. Changing subject, let's look at generosity even though it is commonly omitted in leadership discussions. There is so much need in the world; do something, as a leader to make life better for others. For example, when I was superintendent, we had a young woman who was accepted at Trinity University, something no one from Somerset had ever accomplished, but she lacked money for application; I gave it to her. Later she returned to pay me back, but I told her to do the same for someone else. In other words, give others hope. I am not bragging on myself rather I am emphasizing a little support means the difference in life. Consider being born and reared in a country filled with poverty, human trafficking, sexual assault, hunger, violence and illiteracy.

29. Someone recently asked, "What is the one book everyone should read? Given my propensity against organized religion, I avoided common religious publications. That being said, I responded with The Four Agreements (Ruiz,), an easy and simple read. The author indicated four pillars for life: 1) Don't take it personally; 2) Always do your best; 3) Be impeccable with your words; and 4) Don't make assumptions. When I was in challenging leadership positions, with seemingly no solutions, one or several pillars would solve/help situation. I highly recommend reading and consulting Ruiz's work; on daily basis.

30. Another important leadership commandment is "stand up" for yourself. People commonly look out for themselves, not for someone else. Several personal examples come to mind: 1) As a new AT&T management person, I was transferred to Midland, Texas, not the end of the world, but it could be seen from there. Anyway, during my first week, my boss opened my mail; a disrespectful behavior. I told him, I found opening my mail, insulting and unprofessional; if he wanted to fire me or whatever, do it. He apologized and never did it again.

Another example related to a new home I had built, in Austin. One day after warranty ran out, my foyer ceiling had black mold. I immediately contacted D.R. Horton, builder, and reported the problem. I knew legally they could avoid doing anything because warranty was out, but they sent a crew out to repair it. About two months later, the same problem appeared, but this time it was about 8' long. Horton again sent people out, but could find no moisture leak, so they contracted a mold specialist from Texas Tech University to investigate. He came and spent days checking out everything and reported everything was okay. At this point, I met with Horton's vice president and got him to write a letter indicating, if mold reappeared, company would buy back the house, for what I paid, plus closing costs. He was confident enough to write letter because it appeared everything was fine, but three months later mold reappeared. I took dated pictures and went to see him; he verified mold was back and we set up closing. They paid me, just as letter stipulated. I honestly was shocked, but would buy another Horton home today. The point is, I got my money back because I stood up for myself.

31. An additional poignant, leadership practice involves organizing yourself and desk. Prioritize activities, in terms of importance. Have a "bring up" folder that shifts forward daily and when job comes up, get it done. Obviously scheduling can easily be done on computer, with assistants having access to schedule, when appropriate. Only have one person with capability to add events, other than yourself. I found a "first thing in morning" meeting, with my assistant very helpful; she reminded me of meetings requiring thorough preparation or task completion. No one, other than my boss, interrupted our daily briefing. We were less stressed knowing what and when things were due.

32. Coupled with organization, is the necessity of handling paper one time; we know paper is handled an average of 15 times, if it isn't resolved, at first. Train assistant on what to pass, what to destroy or what to forward. If paper is relevant, it should be date stamped, with office title.

I made decision to reject general email because it consumed time; if it were pertinent, my assistant handled it just like paper. Only my closest subordinates or superior directly emailed me.

33. With consulting firm, I received CEO requests to coach managers who lacked organization. The most extreme time I met with a woman, who literally couldn't be seen because there was so much paper on her desk. I only heard her voice. She literally had trunks full of documents. The first day we worked on her desk, getting rid of irrelevant paper. There was no way she could lead with such a mess in her office/ mind. To some extent, desk and office depict what is going on in brain.

The second day, we conquered two trunks of junk, some of which was years old. She got visibly upset, as we disposed of stuff because she might need it sometime. But, it was impossible to find a document because she had no idea where anything was. I personally think she was psychologically unable to make a decision about what was important and what wasn't.

The final day, we handled, prioritized and delegated paperwork. I stressed three things needed to be on her desk, at day's end: computer, phone and stapler. Nothing is more depressing than coming in the morning and desk is piled with stuff that wasn't managed. My hunch was she reverted to her old self as soon as I left; she probably celebrated when coaching ended or took additional Valium.

Note: Coincidentally I met with a non-government organization director yesterday and her desk, floor and chairs, were covered with paper; obviously, she avoided handling paper one time rather, she spent her time micromanaging. In fact, she couldn't offer me a chair because there was no room or perhaps she didn't want me staying. Smile.

Sidebar: I oppose using in and out baskets because usage postpones decision. I saw lots of managers employing baskets, but I never saw a transformative leader using them.

With that being said, paper is managed, but true leadership comes through people. Once I was flying and the guy next to me asked what I did, so I told him. He then asked what a leader was; my response, "You turn around and if there is no one there, you aren't a leader." In other words, great leaders lead by delegating, even though some find delegating difficult because they fear task won't get done or be quality. Clearly some monitoring is necessary; simply agree on due dates and jointly review work. Provide feedback, both positive and negative and ensure people are valued and respected. P.S. I often asked our folks to review and critique my work; not only did practice improve my work, it fostered their leadership skill sets.

34. Related to feedback, provide both negative and positive. Be sure to use "I" sentences, rather than "you." For example, I like your spreadsheet because it's easy to see data; conversely, I want spreadsheet to be very readable, how might that be done? Feedback must be specific, not some glittering generality.

35. Commonly females receive less negative feedback because some males are afraid "they will cry" so they avoid considered critique, which hinders women from progressing. Indeed, we require feedback to improve.

36. Closely related to feedback, it is imperative to coach leaders up with specific and concise advice. I contemplated over the years what my leadership legacy was; it was mentoring young leaders, by providing encouragement, support and candor. Chairing over 60 doctoral dissertations provided ample opportunity to grow leaders; indeed, many of their careers surpassed my own. I will always be in debt for what students taught me.

37. Oftentimes, females "mess" with their hair when talking; avoid this behavior as it is so distracting.

CHAPTER SEVENTEEN

Oops, I Forgot Several Things

Okay, let's begin summarizing <u>Sunburned Pigs and Other Trivia</u>; I initially spoke to my upbringing, with its strange, yet generally positive aspects. I carefully stressed how important family members were in shaping my life; they clearly made all the difference. My education was addressed, with its strengths and weaknesses, again recognizing how certain people encouraged and guided me. I, then moved to career, where I pointed out capstone successes, as well as screw ups. Finally I discussed leadership commandments, points to consider and to practice. I sincerely hope those portions prove beneficial; remember leaders only succeed when they work and coach others. Don't even think about being the "Lone Ranger; it won't work."

At this point, I elaborate on something different and apart from earlier discussions: physical and emotional health issues. During the last five years, I experienced: heart problems, two knee replacements, both knees simultaneously swelling where walking was impossible, broken hip, total hip replacement, kidney stone, two hand surgeries, stint, three broken wrists, including major wrist surgery, foot surgery and crushed bone holding top teeth in place. There were months of therapy, pain pills, walker, crutches and casts. Many of the health problems related to balance proprisception meaning brain doesn't talk to joints, causing many falls.

Recently, depression set in; I truly felt I had no purpose left in life. But I learned about SARC, Sexual Assault Resource Center, in Bryan, Texas. Fortunately a new class was beginning, consisting of 50 class hours and on the job training and then serving as an advocate for sexual assault, sex trafficking, harassment and bullying survivors. I am so thankful to learn about organization and their mission of service; I now feel, again, I have purpose in life. I chiefly handle the hotline where survivors call and we explain myriad of services for them. We also assist in their setting up "safe plan" in case they are still in harm's way. Plus, we go with them to hospital, for exam, if they want us there for support. Finally we accompany them, should they want us in court. The moral to story is get involved in something bigger than yourself, when depression approaches.

Something else I did in last several months involves pistols. Being a stark liberal, I am basically unsupportive of so many people carrying pistols, but several events occurred in College Station making me wary of living alone, without a firearm. I began the adventure by talking for two hours, with a policeman: 1) Should I buy pistol and learn to shoot? 2) If so, what weapon should I purchase? He convinced me owning and using pistol is good idea and taking requisite training to ensure safety. So, I took Handgun 101 course and bought a Glock 19, generation four pistol. After several days, I decided I loved shooting and took Conceal to Carry test and shooting test and passed with flying colors, in spite of only shooting 9 days. I shot rifles, when I was a kid, but had hardly ever used a pistol. At any rate, I now go to range and shoot daily; you know us Type A's. I love the challenge and sport of shooting; I don't know if I will ever actually carry, but I have the legal option/ skills if necessary.

Pistols…lifelong learning

At this juncture, I want to relate several funny experiences, after major knee surgery. Normally knee replacement patients go home two days, following surgery, but I lost lots of blood. However hospital staff and doctor failed to note how much. During this time, I remember seeing things and talking to invisible people. A Florida friend called and asked how I was doing; I told her the maintenance man did surgery and I was doing great. She said ok and hung up because she thought it was the anesthesia. But three days later an Austin friend came and quickly noted my cognitive skills were gone, so she told nursing staff. When they checked, they realized I desperately needed transfusion. After receiving two pints of blood, I talked and made sense.

After transfusion, they walked me to the shower, my first in five days. The orderly was with me, but when I sat down, the hose was aimed her way and she got drenched. I cracked up laughing, but she didn't think it was so funny. Again, my dark humor.

So, I was released several days later and by then, my Austin friend was gone. I was gimping around on my walker, when I noticed a picture on the floor had fallen over, when I bent over to straighten it up, I lost my balance and landed on the frame, breaking the glass. All the glass went in my butt; how in the hell do you pick glass fragments out of your behind when you can't see it? It wasn't funny then, but I laugh about it now.

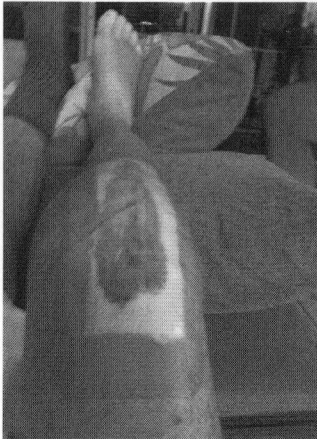

3rd knee surgery in 6 months

CHAPTER EIGHTEEN
That's It Folks!

Pardon the brief digression, but "What's Important?" I experienced lots of political history: two new states, Cuban Missile Crisis, Cold War, Viet Nam War, assassinations of John F. Kennedy, Robert Kennedy, Dr. Martin Luther King, Richard Nixon Resignation, Russian satellite, Man on the Moon, credit cards, Civil Rights legislation, climate change, Affirmative Action, Title IX, Americans with Disabilities Act, Justice Ginsburg, second woman, named to Supreme Court, Hillary Clinton, first female presidential candidate, gay marriage, LGBTQ Movement, Ted Kennedy and John McCain deaths and 9-11-2001. Not only did I live through these historical events, but the advent of technology was amazing: computers, laptops, cell phones, wireless, virtual reality and artificial intelligence.

Given those truly momentous occasions, I still, however, have serious concerns: Lack of respect and empathy for humanity: race, religion, disabilities, gender identification, age, looks, sexual assault, socio-economic-status, meaningful education, sex trafficking, sexual mutilation and torture permeate world.

Another concern is climate change and scattered Republican refusal to accept fact, in spite of melting icebergs, ocean warming, worldwide warming, horrific storms and fires. When topic comes up, naysayers point out weather's cyclical nature to which I agree, but not at the current rate. Perhaps when New Orleans, Boston, San Francisco, and other coastal cities are deluged with water, critics may accept reality. Our global footprint is far too large and our "it's all about me mentality" leads to destruction.

Additionally, there is far too little attention given to climate change; most people appear to believe environment is here for us and what we do to it doesn't matter, not to mention destroying endangered species. It's clearly okay to use a powerful rifle, with enormous scope, to kill exotic species, for trophies. Indeed, we are only a small blemish in world history and far from significant.

My final concern is failure of most people to read critical articles and books; instead, many rely on Facebook, Twitter, Fox News, National Inquirer or whatever. We should examine other points of view, other than our own. We also should participate in public issue forums; indeed, I am taking part on one about feeding the world population. I honestly know little about subject, but I bet I learn from session and others.

In sum, protect and help people, animals and environment. Practice equality and inclusion for all races, gender identities, educations, religions or lack thereof and disabilities. Laugh a lot, especially at yourself. Practice generosity and I do mean practice. Shape legacy by "growing leaders." Make "What's best for students, clients or whomever" the decision making filter. Finally keep in mind leadership is tough, hard, thankless work. **HOW WILL YOU BE REMEMBERED?**

P.S. Behind University of Alabama's football stadium, rests a cemetery. The first tombstone leaves a message I want to use, *Thanks for Stopping By!*

REFERENCES

Gouldner, Alvin. (1957, December), 2. (pp.281-306). Administrative Science Quarterly. "Cosmopolitans and Locals: Toward an Analysis of Latent Social Roles."

Lasswell, Harold. (1936). Editors of Encyclopaedia Brittannica.

Likert, Rensis. (1967). Human Organization: Its Management and Value. New York: McGraw-Hill.

Ruiz, Miguel & Mills, Janet. (2010). Four Agreements. Amber-Allen Publishing Co.

ABOUT THE AUTHOR

Dr. Maria (pronounced Mariah) Shelton received her leadership doctorate, from Texas A&M University. In spite of a wide array of leadership roles: K-12, AT&T, higher education, as well as her own company, she always played a "change agent" role, fostering an active, positive culture, with high expectations. But, by its very nature, "change agents" stir up animosity and angst, creating foes and she truly had those. "No guts, no Glory!"

Maria is a dedicated Texas Aggie who practices generosity, inclusiveness, service, dedication, commitment, loyalty, equality, diversity and humility. A little humor on the last one! She is an active member of A&M's Legacy Foundation, as well as establishing two endowed scholarships for first generation students. In 2012, she was named an Outstanding Alumni, by the College of Education and Human Resources. Her publications, include several books and over 60 refereed journal articles. In addition, she served as president of two national professional organizations, but her most important legacy is mentoring and coaching leaders. Finally, she makes life easier with terrific sense of humor, mostly self-deprecating and love for Stella Marie, her King Charles spaniel.

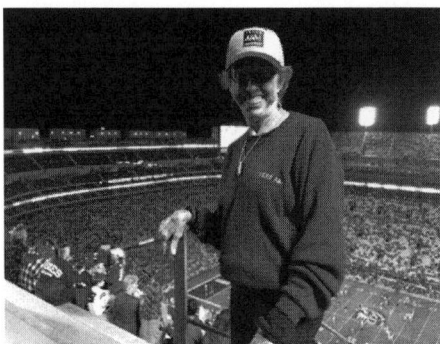

Wow, I was high! Smile

Printed and bound by PG in the USA